# Server

by Ann-Marie Kishel

first step nonfiction

Lerner Publications · Minneapolis

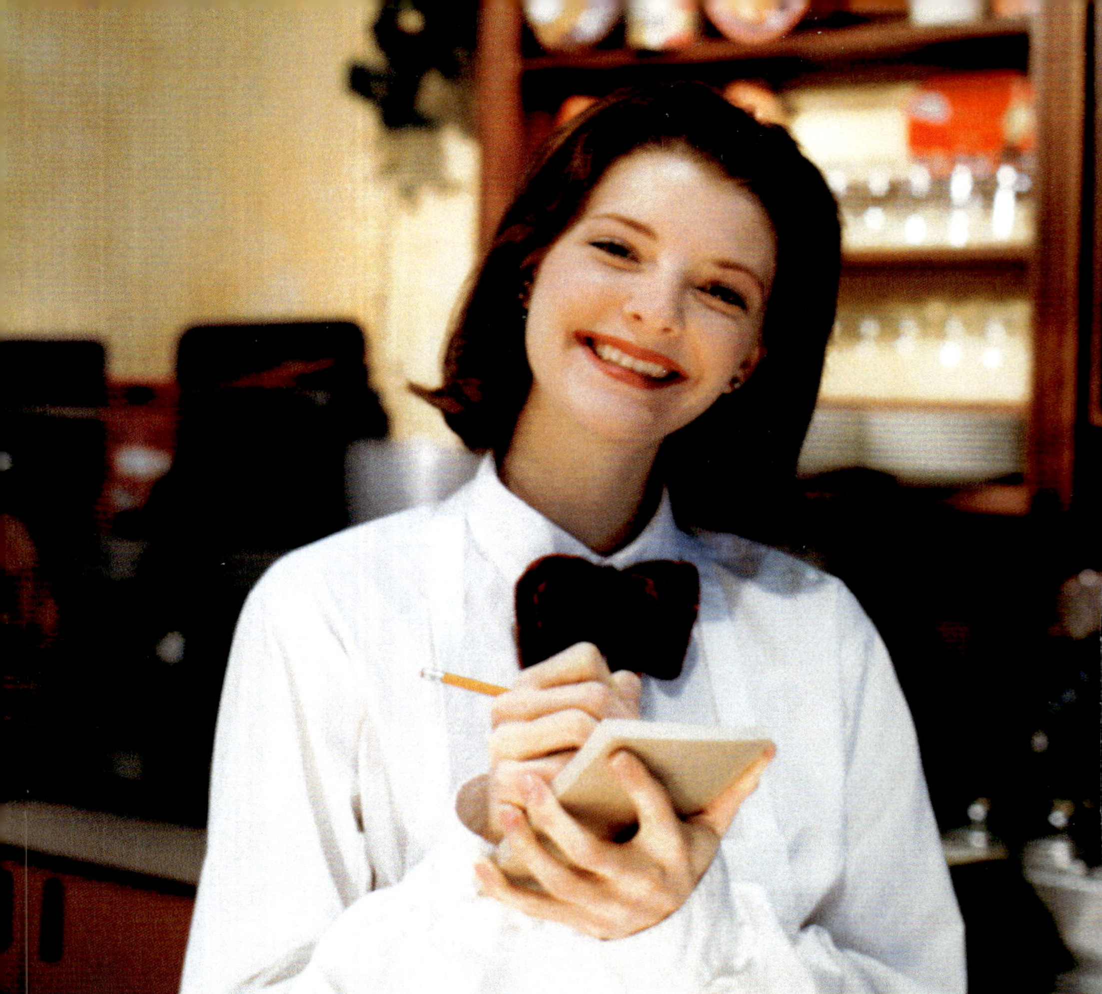

What does a server do?

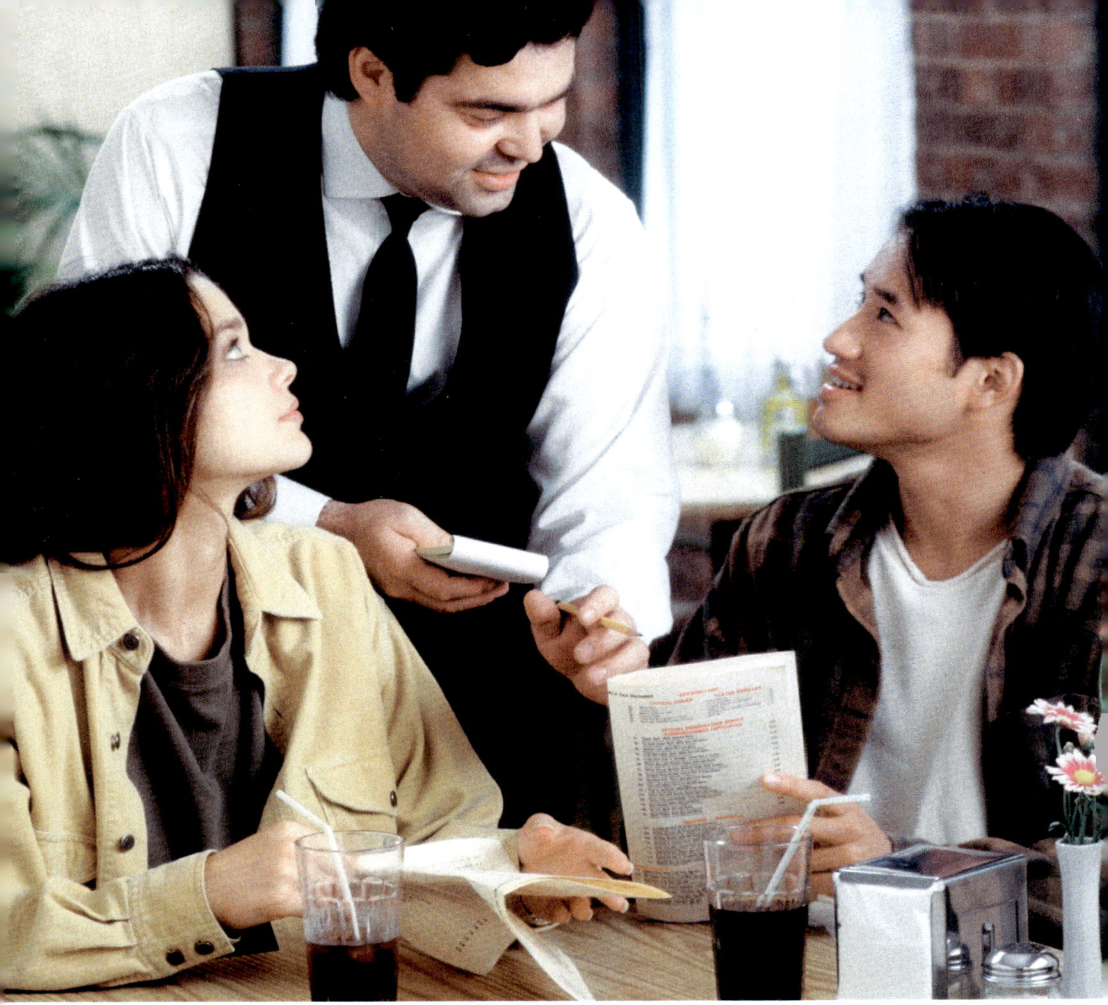

He takes your order.

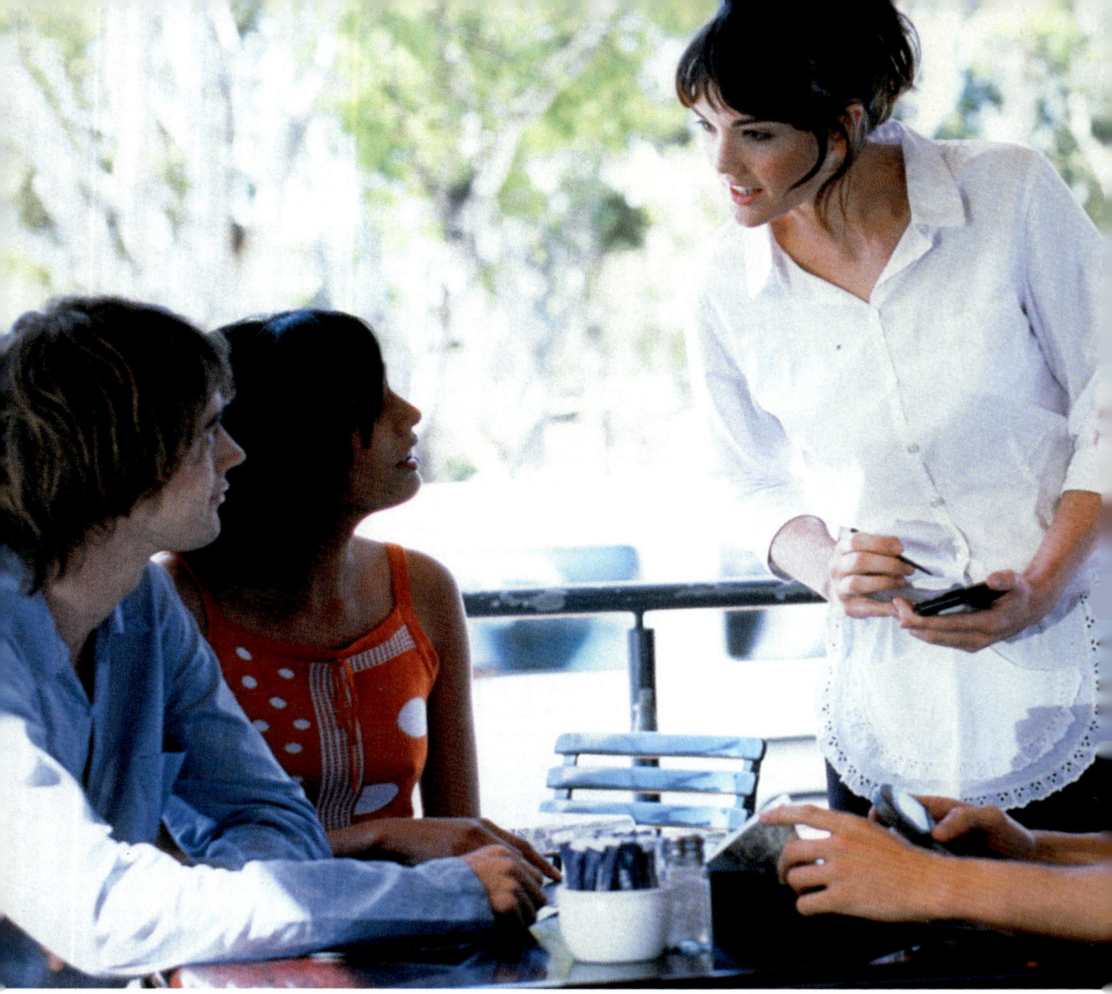

She answers a question.

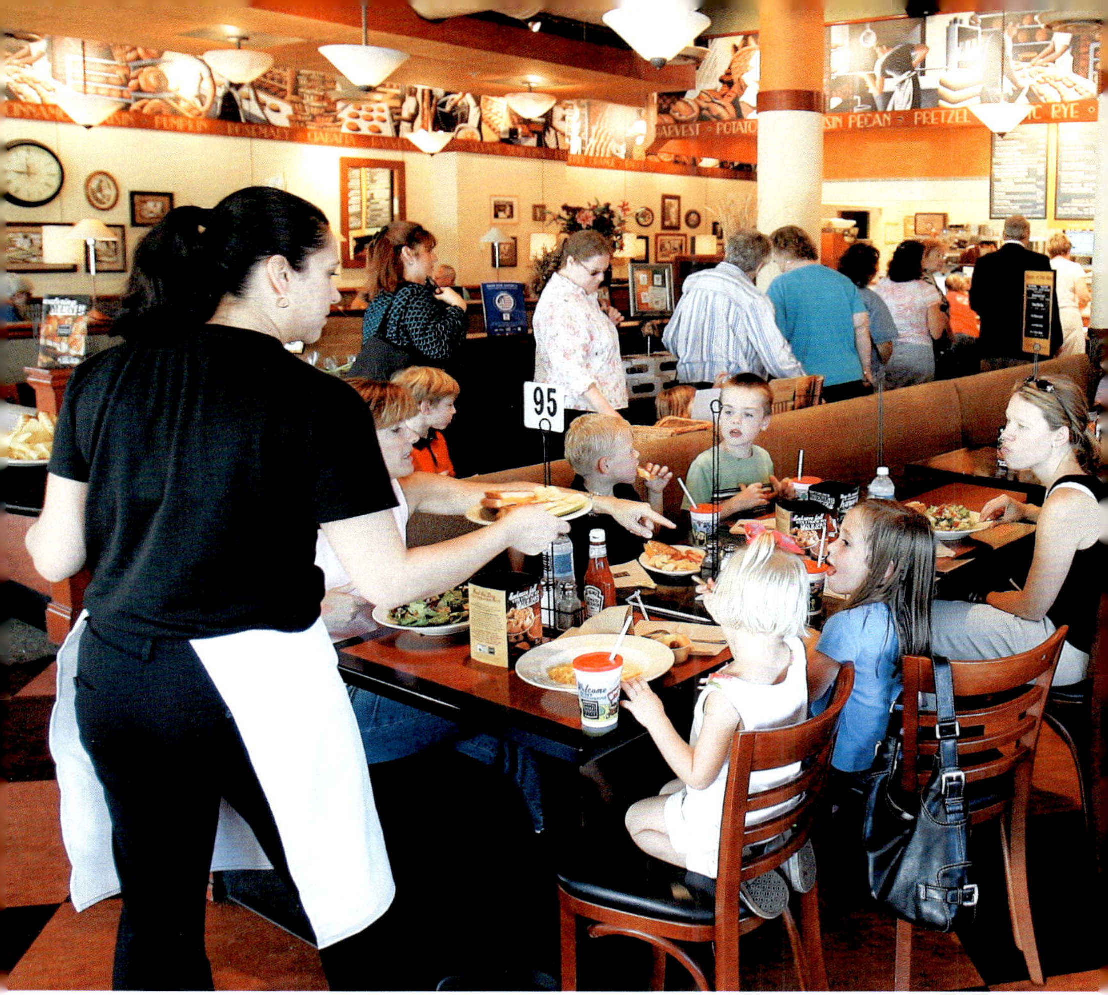


She brings your food.

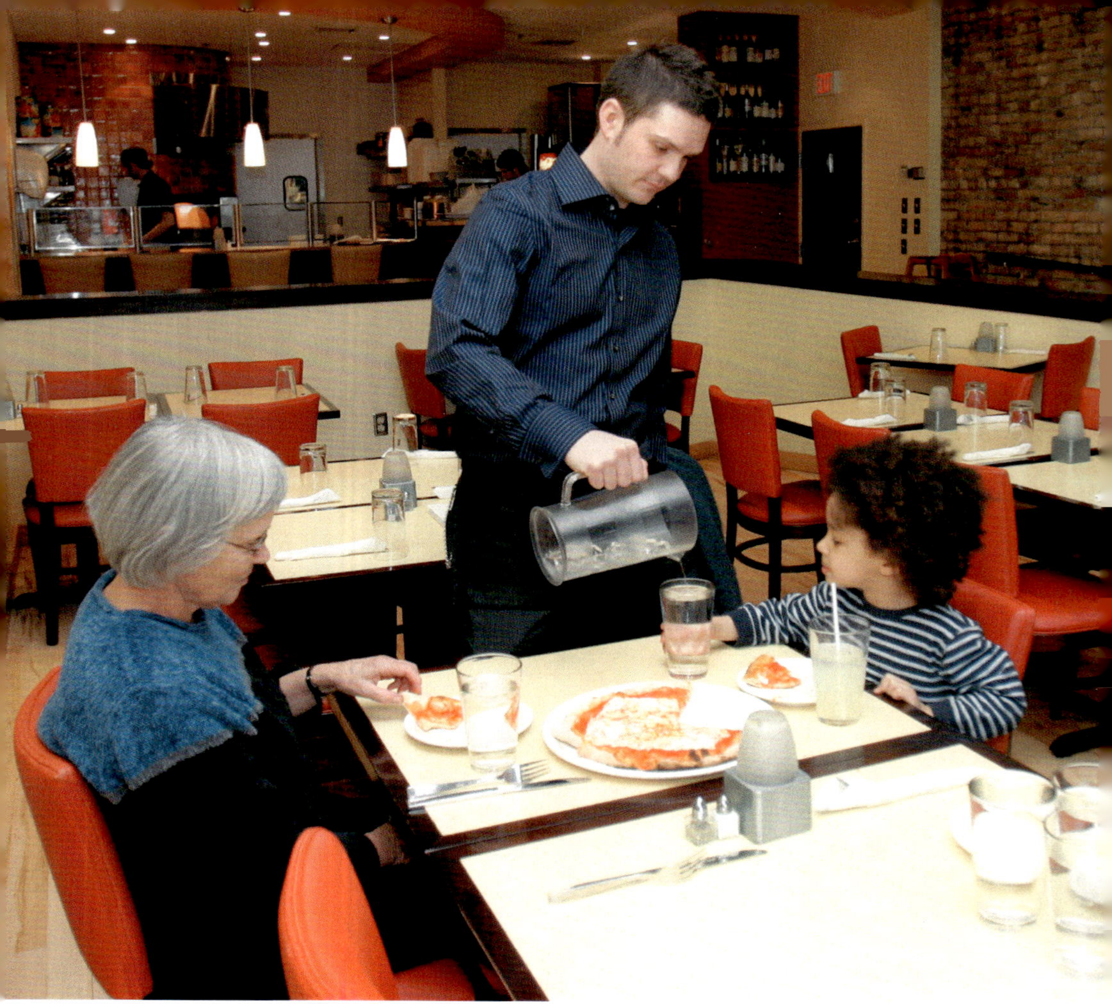

He pours your drink.

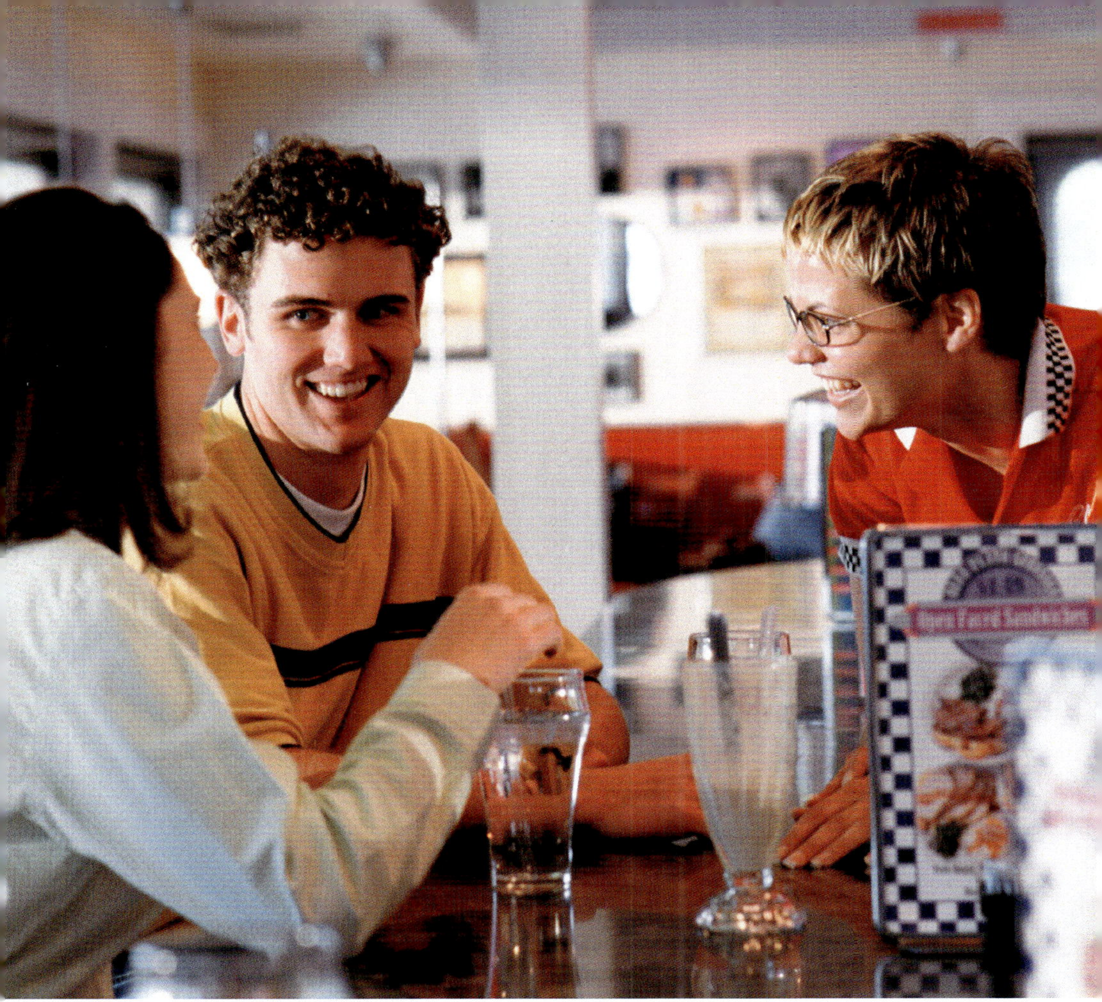


She listens.

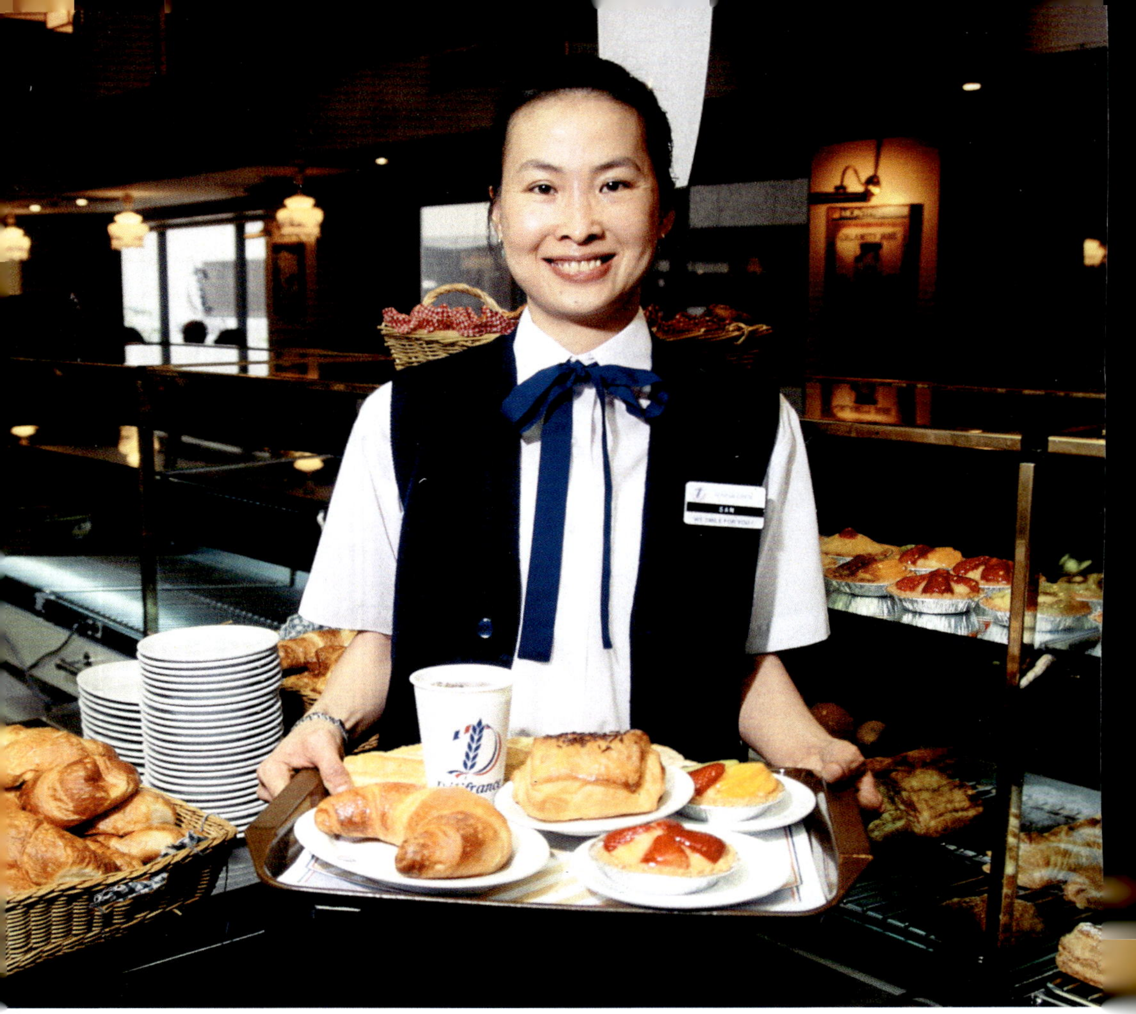

Do you know a server?